HONEST JOHN & GEORGE FOWLER

PRESENT

CAR-TASTROPHES

80 AUTOMOTIVE ATROCITIES FROM THE PAST 20 YEARS

www.veloce.co.uk

First published in September 2016 by Veloce Publishing Limited, Veloce House, Parkway Farm Business Park, Middle Farm Way, Poundbury, Dorchester DT1 3AR, England. Fax 01305 268864 / e-mail info@veloce.co.uk www.veloce.co.uk or www.velocebooks.com. ISBN: 978-1-845849-33-7; UPC: 6-36847-04933-1.

HONEST JOHN & GEORGE FOWLER

PRESENT

CAR-TASTROPHES

80 AUTOMOTIVE ATROCITIES FROM THE PAST 20 YEARS

Contents

Introduction

AUTOMAKERS ARE as prone to turn out clunkers as politicians are to lie. Their cars may be ugly, misconceived, badly built, diabolical to drive, ridiculously thirsty or just plain unreliable. So, which were the worst of the past 20 years? George Fowler, Motoring Editor of *The Daily Star*, gives his opinion from driving an average of two different new cars every week. Honest John tells you what 800,000 letters and emails from readers of *The Telegraph* and his own website have told him. No one else is as qualified to dish out the dirt as these two.

FLAT TYRE RATINGS:

ONE FLAT tyre is dire enough, but five flat tyres is appalling. Two to four flat tyres denote increasingly severe degrees of car-tastrophe.

About the authors

HONEST JOHN wrote the Motoring Agony Column in *The Daily Telegraph* single-handedly for 20 years from January 1995 to January 2015, and started his own website, honestjohn.co.uk, in the year 2000. Having answered around 800,000 letters, e-mails and 'Ask HJ's from *Telegraph* readers and devotees of his own website, he uniquely knows what turns the British public on and off about cars. He has also compiled the world's biggest 'car by car breakdown' of car problem areas at http://www.honestjohn/carbycar/; if you ever want to know 'what could possibly go wrong,' have a look there.

GEORGE FOWLER has been Motoring Editor of *The Daily Star* for the past 20 years, having taken over from the then retired Patrick Mennem in 1996. His first column appeared in a pullout for the British Motor Show at the NEC, which was quickly followed by a small motoring section that turned into half a page in just three months, a full page in one year, and which grew to three pages by 1998. Now that newspapers generally have become smaller it's down to a double-page spread, and George's 'Motor Mouth' column appears every Friday.

Alfa Romeo Brera 3.2 V6
2008

LOVE, BLISS, heaven, joy. That was the way you felt the moment you set eyes on the beautiful Alfa Romeo Brera, especially the 3.2-litre V6. Needless to say, like most red-hot love affairs it didn't last, and the reason for that was although the girl involved may have looked sexy, doing anything even remotely exciting was the last thing on her mind. In fact, after a week spent with the lying little cow I was quite relieved when it was all over. Here was a slitty-eyed 260hp temptress that was supposed to hit 0-62mph in 6.8 seconds on her way to 150mph. Believe me, if it did that the affair would have lasted a lot longer. In fact, it felt like it couldn't out-accelerate a milk float, and as speed is one of the main reasons people buy a car as stunning-looking as the Brera, that's why you don't see many about. It didn't sell. Mind you, there has to be considerably more than just a lack of raciness to put you off a beauty, and the Brera had faults by the body load. For a start, its ponderous 1600kg weight meant that hitting the brakes was like buying a Lottery ticket. Fantastic, but only if you bought the right ticket. Seats with no side supports and a ride best described as variable didn't help either, while the roof was so low, rear seat passengers could only ever get comfortable if they had their heads amputated. The Brera was so thirsty the only people it was likely to keep happy were petrol station owners, and I wouldn't have gone out with this gorgeous creature even if I could have afforded it.

FLAT TYRE RATING:

Austin Rover Mini
1990-2000

NOT THE brilliant, groundbeaking original. Here, we're talking about a car so far past its sell-by date it was as fresh as a 1959 loaf of bread. The final Rover Minis on stupid, ugly, 12-inch wheels were rustbucket junk. Features like the deep door pockets, sliding windows, hinged rear number plate so stuff could be carried on the drop-down boot lid, had all been abandoned. Quality was abysmal, the driving experience was execrable, and the first catalysed Minis were featured on BBC's *Watchdog* because they simply didn't work.

FLAT TYRE RATING: 🛞🛞🛞

Bentley Bentayga
2016

THE BENTLEY Bentgaya. Who's that for? Malaysian monopolists, affluent Arabs, rich Chinese to crash for 'Wrecked Exotics,' tasteless Premier Division footballers and other disgracefully rich bastards and tax exiles who just want to show off. A Ferrari 458, a Lamborghini Aventador or a McLaren P1 at least show some taste. There's an art to building them, and great skill involved in crashing them while under the influence of suspicious substances. The drivers can at least get killed. But nothing, apart from a pink Rolls-Royce Phantom on aftermarket 26-inch wheels, says factory-fresh bling quite as badly as a Bentley Bentgaya. No other car protects its effluent occupants and says what is wrong with society as effectively. I hope the driver of the first Bentley Bentgaya who runs over a starving street kid gets hung, drawn and quartered, or at the very least beaten to death.

GEORGE SAYS: The Bentayga is so massive and so crass it's like having a 30 feet statue of yourself, covered in gold and diamonds, at the entrance to your half a mile long driveway to a house that, while looking a palace, is lit up like a dog track and has so many tasteless ornamental features it could be used as the background set to a movie dedicated to the earth-shattering inventions, ingenuity and genius of Joey Essex's dog.

FLAT TYRE RATING:

BMW 320d M Sport
2015

IT'S THE day every junior rep dreams of. The day his boss walks into the office holding a pair of car keys and tells him to dump his workman-like Nissan and put all his stuff into a shiny brand new BMW. Is this really happening, thinks the overjoyed salesman. Wait until my wife sees this. I'll have to buy a new suit. Little does he know that he is now the proud owner of the one car that the entire sales force had tried and said they'd rather be sacked than ever have to drive again. Welcome to hell, sonny. Why BMW tried to pretend that its 320d rep-mobile was some kind of a supercar beggars belief. Did it think that putting M Sport badges on a 320 diesel, along with 19-inch alloys and racy 35 profile tyres would suddenly turn it into a Ferrari? All that did was turn it from being a perfectly adequate motor into a living nightmare. Big alloys and low profile tyres may look great on a Lamborghini, but all they do on a 320d is turn it into a deafening dunger that's about as comfortable as a concrete hammock. In fact, the 320d M Sport is so loud and uncomfortable, it made the Lamborghini Huracán I had a week later seem like driving a yacht on a millpond. Even on normal road surfaces, it was impossible to drown out the racket by turning on the radio full blast. The only people you're likely to see driving one are probably on their way to the chiropractor to get their backs fixed. Have a 320d, by all means, but for heaven's sake give this one a wide berth.

HJ ADDS: I don't think George quite understands how vital it is for a sales rep to have 19-inch wheels, 35 profile tyres and an 'M Sport' badge on the back of his 2.0-litre BMW diesel. He doesn't have to buy new rims after he potholes them, or ridiculously expensive new tyres every 6000 miles, and he can get a whoopee cushion to protect his coccyx when visiting clients in the country. It's *Telegraph* readers who get hoodwinked into these stupid wheels and tyres, and half a dozen write to me every week asking what they can do to improve the ride quality of their idiotic M Sport diesels. You wouldn't send a builder to work in ballet shoes, so if you fit racing tyres to a boggo family saloon it's never going to work.

FLAT TYRE RATING: 🛞🛞🛞🛞🛞

BMW X6
2008-2014

THIS ISN'T included because it is a fundamentally bad car. It's here because of the concept behind it and the blingers who buy it. Someone at BMW must have decided that their X5 SUV was not sufficiently intimidating for German autobahns, and that something altogether more menacing was required. So they threw away any vestige of practicality, decapitated an X5 and dropped a coupé-like roof onto it, clearly indicating that the one and only purpose of the X6 was to frighten and bully every other vehicle into submission. And this has proved to be the case on motorways when the blinding lights just behind your rear bumper turn out to be the Xenons of an X6; in cities where they indiscriminately shoulder you aside; on roundabouts where they always have right of way, and emerging from side roads where they simply pull out as if saying, "What are you going to do about it?" And surprisingly, though four-wheel drive, they are fatal at traction in the snow. The X6 in the picture simply slid off the road into a snowdrift. Yet, unlike a Land Rover, it was unable to summon a small arsenal of gripping aids. It just sat there spinning its wheels until another X6 hauled it out.

GEORGE SAYS: The X6 is the perfect sledgehammer for people who believe that no one should be driving on *their* road. Trouble is, it's so ugly beyond belief, that all it does is prove how utterly tasteless and vulgar it is. Mind you, if you found one upside down in a canal you couldn't mistake it for an abandoned shopping trolley. You'd think it was an upturned barge.

FLAT TYRE RATING: 🛞🛞🛞

Cadillac CTS 2.8
2004-2008

It must have seemed so tempting. Here was a good-looking, quick, well-equipped, beautifully kitted out motor at a price that seemed like it should have cost considerably more. In fact, here's what General Motors, under its British name of Vauxhall, said about it when it went on sale in the UK: "It's a true luxury sports saloon with a European driving feel." And here's what I added: "Whatever you do, however much you're tempted, don't buy one." Why not? Let's start with the auto box that was always in two minds when you chose 'sport,' or was so single-minded in 'auto' that it kept continually shifting gear or simply refusing to change and dying in auto. Then there was its, er, heating settings. You may have been able to set it at any temperature you fancied but the result was the same. You either boiled to death or froze to death. Meanwhile, driver and passengers were deafened by a series of warning buzzers for just about everything from the keys, doors, buckle (safety belt catch in Europe) and even the 'trunk' (Brits know this as a boot). Worse than that, while this cacophony was assaulting your ears, the speedo was reading in kph rather than miles per hour. Meanwhile Cadillac's 'sporty' 2.8-litre V6 sounded like a cat scrabbling for grip on a corrugated tin roof; it produced as much pull as an Under 11 Girls Tug of War team, and drank petrol like it was coming out of an overflowing reservoir. Apart from that, though, it was genuinely awful.

FLAT TYRE RATING: 🛞

Cadillac Seville
1998-2004

STUPID IDEAS aren't just the domain of barmy boffins and burglars who post pictures on the internet of themselves with their stolen loot. Oh no, car companies are more than capable of coming up with their own half-baked schemes. And boy did General Motors come up with a cracker when it decided to make a right-hand drive version of the Cadillac Seville and sell it in the UK. It probably thought that Brits would jump at the chance of driving around in a mixture of cream leather, real wood trim, and a 4.6-litre V8 that, in 2004, made the Seville the fastest front-wheel-drive car in the world at the time. Needless to say it was wrong. The Seville may have been quick and quiet, but it was so ugly it would have beaten a dustbin lorry to first prize in an eyesore contest. The front looked like a drain trap and there was so much rear overhang it would have kept an elephant dry. Is that it? No it's not. For such a huge car, rear legroom was pitiful and, in Britain, where the sales experts at Vauxhall got the odious job of selling the thing, they refused to give any fuel consumption figures. I did my own and found that the Seville was gulping down petrol at just 12.8mpg even at a steady 30mph. In fact, this car was so good at it that it set a whole new record. It beat my previous instant worst fuel consumption figure of 2mpg (set in a Jeep Grand Cherokee going flat out up a Scottish hill in second gear) by displaying the figure nought. Zero mpg will never be beaten.

HJ ADDS: The 1984 Cadillac Seville Eleganza 'humpback' (top right) with velour interior was condemned on the TV show *Fast n' Loud* as a car for having sex in with prostitutes.

Thanks for that, Honest.

FLAT TYRE RATING: 🛞🛞🛞

Chevrolet Captiva
2007-2015

IT'S NOT good when friends fall out but sometimes there's no avoiding it. The particular friend I'm thinking about as I write this is the very same Honest John who partnered me in this book, and there's no way to sugar the pill ... he lied to me. We were in Ireland in 2006, and he was driving the then new Chevrolet Captiva, when he suddenly pulled up and said: "It's your turn to drive." Well, I'm sorry, Honest, but it certainly was not. We normally drive for a couple of hours each before swapping seats, and he'd only been behind the wheel for 20 minutes. The row that followed was not nice to hear but, basically, it centred on an agreement we'd had about whose turn it was NOT to drive the Captiva. That's how bad it was. Neither of us wanted to be behind the wheel, but to be fair, it was pretty rotten being in the passenger seat, too, as this horrible excuse for a family seven-seater bumped and lurched its way from Cork to the Atlantic coast with all the charm of the top deck of a '70s school bus, and an interior that looked like it had been visited by thieves, there were that many holes in it where switches and expensive kit had been removed. It was bouncy, lifeless, had a dreadful gearbox and dull steering. Still, there were two good things that happened on that trip. First, a friend suddenly got a text from me THREE DAYS after I sent it, while we were in a pub on the Atlantic coast. While it seems like you have to wait until the cows come home for something to happen in Ireland, the second thing that happened was that the Captiva got kicked to pieces on a country lane by a herd of cows on their way to be milked. Oh, the joy of hearing each hoof land right on target. Still, the Captiva had been asking for it.

FLAT TYRE RATING: 🛞 🛞 🛞 🛞

Chrysler Neon
1999-2005

IT WOULD be far quicker to tell you what was right with the Chrysler Neon than what was wrong. So here we go ... it looked good and it was cheap. When it first arrived in Europe in 1999, its American owners thought they were on to a winner, but they hadn't taken into account the rapidly rising standards of cars not just from Europe, but from Asia too. People were getting fussy about their motors, and while the Neon may have looked good and started at £11,000 for what was a fair-sized motor, you only had to drive it for a minute to realise that it wasn't anywhere near the bargain that Chrysler were claiming it was. Its 2.0-litre engine, with 136hp, was noisy and underpowered, it handled like a trampoline, there was hardly any room for rear seat passengers – despite its size – and equipment features included wind-up windows for those unlucky enough to be wedged into the back of it. Worse still, the American Insurance Institute for Highway Safety gave it their worst possible rating of "poor" and described it as a "disaster." The second generation Neon gained wood and leather trim in top models, but it was so obviously stuck on at the last minute it wouldn't have impressed a schoolboy. Some structural changes saw it move up to the second worst insurance category of 'marginal,' but by then the damage had been done. The average age of Neon buyers was 53, and it drove like a car whose owners couldn't care less how bad it was, as long as it was cheap. Chrysler finally nailed down the lid on it in 2005.

FLAT TYRE RATING: 🛞 🛞 🛞 🛞

Chrysler PT Cruiser convertible
2005-2008

YOU CAN see the thinking. "We've got this retro hatchback MPV that looks like a 1952 Ford Prefect, so let's customise it into a cabrio." You can figure why Ford, having cut the top off its Prefect in the late 1930s, didn't try the same thing again in 1952. In the UK it came with a 2.4-litre four-cylinder engine and usually a four-speed automatic transmission, so was no ball of fire, and the promise of a five-seater convertible wasn't met because the hood irons took up too much space. Almost every review contains the word 'bad,' even when qualified with 'not too.' It was tagged onto the launch of the 300C Touring in Glasgow, and the only three good things about that were Stornoway black pudding, it didn't rain, and no one got shivved.

GEORGE ADDS: When the second generation Cruiser arrived in 2005, it was a huge improvement, but it would have been almost impossible to have made it any worse. Chrysler now offered a Mercedes-made 2.2-litre diesel with 121hp backed up by a colossal 300Nm of torque. It was so superior to the noisy, gutless, charmless 140hp, 2.0-litre petrol engine that it did make it a lot better to drive, but being better than rubbish is still not even approaching good, and as the whole thing weighed a ridiculous 1613kg (3549lb) it felt like the cabin was connected to the chassis by marshmallow. It was about as communicative as a teenager on a Sunday morning. Chrysler claimed the rear seats were removable and, indeed, they were, but they were so heavy I couldn't lift them back in, so left them by the side of the car for Chrysler to pick up, probably with the aid of a crane.

FLAT TYRE RATING: 🛞🛞🛞

Chrysler Sebring sedan
2006-2010

ONE OF the instantly rotten, now forgotten fruits of the ill-fated merger between what they insisted on calling 'Dime-ler Chrysler,' it was a truly appalling crock of characterless crap that wasn't even reliable. Mercedes-Benz UK used to have a great American boss called Joe Eberhardt, who got on really well with its excellent PR Geoff Day, and ran a happy ship selling everything from Smart ForTwos to S600Ls. But then they shipped out the pair to rescue Chrysler USA, and I remember an embarrassed Joe returning to the UK and having to go on stage in a duet with some Chrysler guy at the 2006 British Motor Show press conference to launch this instant junker. It didn't look good, it didn't drive well, it didn't handle, it wasn't economical, it wasn't reliable, and it didn't sell. Though if you had specified a convertible for your Californian 'fly-drive,' and you were really unlucky, you could suffer the misery of having one foisted on you at the rental desk. Death Valley in one of these disasters truly was hell on wheels.

FLAT TYRE RATING: 🛞🛞🛞🛞

Chrysler Delta
2011-2014

THE BIGGEST surprise about the so-called 'Chrysler' Delta is that it managed to stagger on from 2011 to 2014 in the UK. How owner FIAT thought it could put a Chrysler badge on a Lancia, give it the ride of an old folks' home, the price of a *real* home and cover it in plastic is a mystery. Of course, people knew it was a Lancia. The brand was infamous for rusting so much that all Lancias were withdrawn from sale in the UK in 1994, but the famous Delta name had continued, and that wasn't changed. Now free from major rust problems it looked, on the surface, to be a good car when it went on sale. It was good-looking, surprisingly roomy and extremely comfortable. Trouble was, nearly all the smart silver-and-black knobs, door trim and even the cloth-like door inserts turned out to be plastic. The door pockets were far too skinny and, while the centre console had a cooled section for bottles, you couldn't find a bottle small enough to fit in it. That meant you couldn't shut the lid, which in turn switched on the cooling system, so your tiny but still over-sized bottle of cold water quickly warmed up. If ever there was a car for old people with lots of money and no brains, this was it.

FLAT TYRE RATING: 🛞🛞🛞

Citroën C3 Pluriel
2003-2010

REMEMBER THE Rubik's Cube? It was all the rage in the 1970s, and I learned how to solve it. I couldn't, however, for the life of me work out how to put a Pluriel back together. This fiendish invention had a folding roof and, I kid you not, a revolving rear window, all controlled by a barmy five separate release mechanisms which needed another five buttons to get them to spring into action. I took it all apart and had to phone Citroën for help to put it back together. The drive wasn't much use either, as the wind threatened to blow you out of the car, the noise left you deafened, and the ride was like being on a fairground rocking horse. Meanwhile, a lot of cheap plastic helped keep the price down, but turned the interior into a roadside cafe. I have, however, left the worst until last. If you wanted a full fresh air experience you had to remove the roof and side bars altogether and put them in the ... house. There was no stowage area big enough for them, so you had to appeal to the heavens before you went out in it. Clouds don't listen to prayers.

HJ SAYS: The Citroën Pluriel might have worked in a different climate. Imagine a modern version of the plastic 2CV based Citroën Mehari as a sort of surfer's pick-up with a drop-down tailgate that could be converted back into a car at the end of the season to keep out the rain. Except seasons don't work like that in the UK. And the seals between the Pluriel's roof hoops didn't keep out the rain. Then, of course, all that open area with lack of support meant the body was more prone to twist than Chubby Checker. It was as much a flexible friend as an Access card. It was also one of the first Citroëns with an optional automated manual gearbox called Sensodrive that, like the Addams Family, involved a lot of Lurch.

FLAT TYRE RATING:

Citroën DS4
2011

AFTER THE huge, well-deserved success of the Citroën DS3 came this misconceived mess. Part-hatchback, part-coupé, part-'crossover,' part-handbag, it came on stiff suspension, huge wheels and ridiculous low profile tyres. Worse than that, this hard-riding horror was the antithesis of the superbly smooth Citroën DS, a car so advanced in its day it made every other car feel like a cart. Its saving grace was an expensive optional leather interior that might have been designed for Madame Boviney. However, I've saved the most crass to the last. While we were inspecting the car on its plinth in a specially-built pavilion outside the W Hotel in Barcelona, a colleague named Massimo Pini pointed out that the rear door windows didn't go down. A sheepish Citroën stylist admitted over dinner that in order for the windows to come to a point at the back, he couldn't make them retract. The next day, while filming the DS4, one of its pointlessly pointed rear door windows stabbed me in the cheek, leaving a lasting impression.

FLAT TYRE RATING: 🛞 🛞 🛞 🛞

Daewoo Nexia
1995-1997

I HAVE a wonderful recipe for porridge. What you do is pour half a cup of extra large ground oats and a whole cup of unsweetened Alpro into a big Pyrex bowl, and shove it into the microwave for three minutes. Then you take it out, stir it, and put it back into the microwave for a further two minutes. The result is a thick, glutinous mass that semi-solidifies as it cools, and if it were a car it would drive like the Daewoo Nexia. This was basically the 1984-1991 Vauxhall/Opel Astra E or Belmont, assembled in South Korea, re-jigged with 1.5-litre GM motors, loaded with kit like ABS and air-con, and sold on the 'Daewoo deal' with three years servicing included in the price. Prone to electrical failures, melting GF50 timing belt pulleys, and the extremely expensive demise of its ABS, by autumn 2015 only 245 were left on Britain's roads, which was 245 too many. By now, the last few which still ran should have been smashed to bits in destruction derbies. Their endings could not have come too soon.

FLAT TYRE RATING: 🛞🛞🛞🛞

37

Daewoo Kalos
2002-2004

IN AN effort to appeal to an elderly market, Daewoo made the suspension of the Kalos so soft that the car was afraid of corners. Its tyres would squeal loudly in fear at the merest hint of a change of direction. The short-lived attempt at inflicting this on the unsuspecting aged, was both cynical and 'kalos.' Buyers thought they got a lot for their seven grand: five three-point seatbelts, power steering, ABS, a remote switched alarm, a 1.4 engine, three years warranty and even an Institute of Advanced Motorists assessment thrown in. Torque steer was also provided in good measure, from a car with only 123Nm torque. Buyers could have gone the whole hog (or should that be 'the whole dog?') and bought the 93hp 1.4 16v automatic for just under ten grand, and robbed their grasping grandchildren of three grand's worth of deposit on a flat, but that just wouldn't have been fair.

FLAT TYRE RATING: 🛞🛞🛞

Dodge Caliber
2006-2010

"NOW THERE'S an idea." I wrote ten years ago. "A car that drives like a truck." Actually, the basic idea was quite good, as the proliferation of 'Sport Utility Vehicle Crossovers' has proven. As far as I can remember, it all began with the very basic Toyota Kijang two-wheel drive utility car in Indonesia in the 1970s, then progressed via the Isuzu Panther, and most successfully the Nissan Qashqai, to more than a hundred high-riding hatchbacks that are currently on sale. Everyone, it seems, wants to see over hedges and look down on people in Fiestas. In the Dodge Caliber you sat up, and the huge steering wheel was right in your face with no reach adjustment, so you had to keep the thing close to your chest. Just like driving a Nissan Navara or a Mitsubishi L200 or an Isuzu Rodeo. You got massive wheels, with chunky 215/55 R18 tyres that smashed their way through potholes and over speed humps. Essentially, everything that a BMW X5 had, except four-wheel drive, decent suspension, and any status at all. Undulating roads sent the springs into floatation mode. And those massive, kerb-crunching 18-inch tyres were so stiff they torque-steered and tramlined on hard acceleration. In its favour, at prices from £11,495 it was cheap for a Jeep.

FLAT TYRE RATING:

FIAT 500L MPW TwinAir
2013

I CAN'T blame FIAT for squeezing everything it can out of the success of the FIAT 500, but squeezing seven people into this ungainly vehicle, then expecting a two-cylinder 875cc engine to pull them along just wasn't on and doesn't work. Neither does the suspension that, like a pick-up truck's, makes it rock hard and bouncy with just two aboard. Happily, the FIAT 500L Trekking with a 1.6 diesel engine is a lot better, fitted with a trick diff and Goodyear Vector 4 Seasons tyres to help prevent it drifting into snowdrifts. 80% of FIAT's entire production is now labelled '500,' which is milking the company's single success far too much. An additional danger is that the basic 500 is long overdue for a restyle and, while this could be done brilliantly in the land of style, it's so important to FIAT that, inevitably, committee after committee, and research after research will turn it into a compromise that everyone apart from the stylists reluctantly agree on, and which then ultimately flops.

FLAT TYRE RATING: 🛞🛞

FIAT Multipla
2000-2010

THIS WAS nuts. Completely loony looking, with strange lights that gave it the appearance of a cross between a frog and a snail. Like the mad 'concept' cars you sometimes see at motor shows, yet this one somehow made production. I loved it. Never mind the rubberised trim that rubbed off under your fingers, or the side windows that bowed outwards at more than 100mph. It seated six comfortably in two rows of three. It had a decent enough 1.9-litre diesel engine (or a less enticing 1.6 petrol). Photographers bought them and ferried models to location shoots. At least, the first generation of Multipla showed that some Italians had a sense of humour. The second generation 'face-lift' revealed that FIAT management didn't. "Okay, you've all had your fun with things like rear window stickers that read 'Wait until you see the front.' Now it's time to inflict some corporate blandness on the thing and pretend that we aren't Italian at all."

GEORGE SAYS: The original Multipla, with the bulging face of a frog that had received an electric shock, was so ugly I was genuinely embarrassed to be seen in it. Most of its drivers were mums with lots of children who drove past smiling as if they'd just discovered they were pregnant again. The only time Mr Husband ever got behind the wheel was when the family went on holiday, because the Uglipla was actually quite practical. Worst thing that happened to me was when I took one to Asda and a woman driving out of the car park smiled and waved at me so intensely it was if she'd discovered a long lost pet. I just wanted to crawl out of the car and never come back.

FLAT TYRE RATING:

FIAT Doblo Family
2001-2009

DESIGN BRIEFING: "Okay, it's a van. Vans are practical. They are driven by the lowest level of driver, 95% of whom don't own them. So we can think like Americans. Deliberately make the Doblo as ugly as possible, just as long as it can carry a huge amount of stuff. And we can cut some windows in the sides and shove seven seats in for Catholic families. Then stick a 1248cc diesel engine under the bonnet so it won't go too fast and kill them. I'm getting excited. This will be the complete antithesis of Italian design. Ugo Zagato, Alfredo Vignale and Sergio Pininfarina will turn in their graves. What's that? You all resign? Okay, I'll give the design brief to my kids."

FLAT TYRE RATING:

Ford Probe 24v
1994-1998

I'LL SAY one thing for the Ford Probe. It didn't half look good. Oh, and the 2.5-litre 24 valve V6 I drove in 1997 sounded fantastic. Now I'll say some other things. It was such a huge disappointment, it turned out to be one of my all time letdowns. For power read zero, until you got it going, by which time you'd already reached another time zone. For comfort read zero, because the steering wheel was so thin it seemed to have been nicked from a '60s Cortina and, anyway, your knees got in the way because the driver's seat was so badly positioned it felt like you were sitting in a space rocket waiting to take off. All the time your bum hurt by being so low down and squashed and, even if you could see where you were going the headlights were about as much use as a candle. For interior design read, you guessed it, zero. Its instruments were scattered haphazardly around a cheapo plastic dash and nearly all of them were sited so low down you had to take your eyes off the road even to read the clock. For quietness it gets, er, zero, unless you found yourself driving down a road surfaced with butter, and you couldn't drown out the racket with the radio, because for most of the time it didn't work. What more could be wrong? Well as that covers the entire car, there's really nothing left to complain about.

FLAT TYRE RATING: ⚙⚙⚙⚙⚙

48

Ford Fusion
2002-2012

WHAT REALLY puzzles me about the Fusion is that Ford managed to sell so many. Since driving it in 2003, I've never even been remotely tempted by the awful prospect of stepping into another. In fact, Ford also seemed so bored with it that, despite producing this small garden shed on wheels for ten long and dreary years the only time it updated it was in 2005, and that was just to make 'cosmetic' changes. The Fusion+ (with a plus sign) that Ford loaned to me was uncomfortable, cramped, slow, drove like a pudding, and gave a new meaning to the word 'enjoyment' that Ford used in adverts for it. The Fusion was only enjoyable when it was parked in the garage, because that way you didn't even have to look at it, never mind drive it. For starters, it was nigh on impossible to get comfy in a Fusion. The front seats had a weird balloon-shaped section in the middle of them which left you feeling as if you were sitting on top of a crushed bag of jellies, while hapless drivers had to sit far too close to the non-reach-adjustable steering wheel if they wanted their feet to reach the pedals, which always helps. Ford claimed there was room for three passengers in the back, but when my wife and I went on a day trip with three kids sitting behind us they were extremely unhappy, and never stopped telling us how cramped and uncomfortable they were. These days the only place you're likely to see a Fusion is in the disabled bay at a supermarket.

HJ ADDS TO THE CONFUSION TO POINT OUT THAT: the Fusion was a station wagon version of the Fiesta aimed at the mobility market, who were happy with anything they could get a wheelchair into the back of without lifting it over a sill. The raised suspension, that destroyed the Fiesta's decent handling, made it easier for the elderly to get in and out.

FLAT TYRE RATING:

Ford Racing Puma
2001

AS DISASTERS go, the Ford Racing Puma was right down there with the *Titanic*. Take one perfectly good car, cover it with go-faster stripes, add a noisy, tunnel-sized car accessory shop exhaust, wide alloys under big wheelarches, spend as little as possible on the engine, add £10,000 to the price and wait for the mugs to roll in. It didn't work. At a staggering £23,000 the Racing Puma was a massive letdown, to say the least. Changes to its 1679cc motor included tinkering with the camshafts and engine management system to give it a power increase of just 30hp, to 155hp, while a pathetic torque figure of 162Nm left it seriously bereft of any pulling power until it reached the stage where you expected the cylinder head to fly through the bonnet. Added to that, its handling ability at speed was so scary it felt like the car was being shaken by an invisible giant hand, as it rattled and shuddered with so much violence you expected the whole thing to collapse into a boiling heap of broken coils and springs. Ford said it was limiting production to just 1000 Racing Pumas, but sold fewer than 500 in the end.

FLAT TYRE RATING:

Honda City
2002-2006

IN THEIR infantile wisdom, car marketing departments in Thailand rejected small hatchbacks like the brilliant original Toyota Yaris and Honda Jazz because they thought Thais needed a boot behind them. So the Yaris was turned into the perfectly decent Soluna Vios saloon with a 110hp 1.5VVTi engine and (usually) a four-speed autobox, but the Jazz was rebodied into the stylistic excrescence of the Honda City. Happily, sense soon prevailed, and Thailand got the Jazz, which it welcomed with open arms and even its own custom car magazine. Toyota followed with the 2005 second-generation Yaris. And, while the Soluna Vios still chugged along nicely, the Jazz based Honda City floundered. It was dropped like a hot stone and replaced with the nicely proportioned 120hp 1.5 iVTEC 2nd generation Jazz-based City, complete with a five-speed autobox (as in the Thai Jazz). But, like a fart in a lift, the 2002 shape Jazz City simply wouldn't go away, because they refused to break down. Consequently, the city streets of Thailand are still polluted by Honda Citys. A pair of them lurk across the soi from our house in Bang Kruay, necessitating closure of curtains. Years later (2014) Thai stylists stuck a boot on the back of their Hyundai i10-sized Honda Brio, and turned it into the horrible mess that was badged 'Amaze.'

FLAT TYRE RATING: 🛞🛞

Hummer H2
2003-2009

THE AMERICANS invented the brilliant Jeep and put it into production just in time to save the world in 1941. It was so good that Rover copied it, stuck a Rover 60 engine in, clad it in surplus WW2 aluminium and called it the Land Rover. But when the Yanks needed another all-purpose military vehicle they went right over the top and created the eight foot wide Hummer H1. A lot of people wanted one. People like Arnold Schwarzenegger. Don King gave one to Frank Warren. "What's that tinkling noise?" Frank allegedly said, while driving his down a London side street. "It's the door mirrors you're ripping off the cars parked either side," replied a passenger. So the Hummer people came up with a slightly narrower one called the H2, which had a standard roof rack made of iron girders. I found one jammed against the air-con ducting in an underground car park, so suggested to the driver that he used the automatic tyre pressure reducing function to lower it. But this feature wasn't carried over from the H1 to the H2, so he stayed stuck.

FLAT TYRE RATING:

Hyundai Accent
2000-2006

IN THE year 2003, the hideous Hyundai Accent came close to achieving something no other car had got even near to doing. It became the worst car I'd ever driven since the disastrous Tata Safari, which I described as "vile beyond belief." Here was a car that was so mind-bogglingly slow and tedious you'd only want to see it being driven by politicians, tax inspectors or health and safety workers. The Accent's mighty 8-valve 1.3-litre "power-train" (Hyundai's words) with a massive 83hp, saw it hit 0-60mph in 13 seconds and go on to 108mph. At least, that was the claim. In reality it would be time for bed by the time it got even over 85mph, and anyway, no Accent owners would ever take it beyond 60mph. It made my wife's 13-year-old Ford Fiesta seem like a supercar. Worst thing was coming to a hill, well, a slight incline, when the Accent really began to struggle, and you'd have to change down a gear to stop pedestrians from walking past. The interior, described by Hyundai as "fresh, clean and modern," was an old-fashioned, cheap and cheerless sea of variable-coloured plastic, the accessory shop radio was a fiddly affair that needed fingers like knitting needles to make it work, and, although it was begging to be nicked, nobody in their right mind would have wanted it. The ride was wrecked by a huge V-shaped crease in the bonnet, that appeared to swing around in front of you every time you took a bend, making you feel dizzy. It did have one good point, though. You could get out and walk away when your journey was over.

HJ ADDS: It was on the launch of this particular car in the Bordeaux region of France that we stopped for a meal involving truffles in St Emilion, and I noticed a placard outside one of the tourist eateries announcing: "English spoken, with a French accent."

FLAT TYRE RATING: 🛞 🛞 🛞 🛞 🛞

Hyundai Trajet
2000-2004

NO ONE can resist a bargain, so Hyundai thought it would cram its big people carrier, the Trajet, with lots of goodies, add a V6 motor, make it four grand cheaper than an excellent SEAT Alhambra, and a massive £10,000 less than a Renault Espace. Well, it didn't work. The Trajet was quickly nicknamed 'the Tragic' by motoring scribes who were less than impressed, despite its air-con, cruise control, massive electric sunroof, and even heated electric door mirrors, which were a bit fancy for the year 2000, all as standard fittings. In fact, I really hadn't worked out exactly why I hated it until I smashed it up by reversing into a three-feet-high metal post at my local tip at 10mph. I couldn't believe the damage, or work out why I suddenly felt happy, rather than angry. Then I realised. It was its noisy, irritating engine, with all the power of a one volt battery, its stupidly uncomfortable seating position, its notchy and clumsy auto gearbox, and its disastrous roly-poly ride, which just made passengers riding in this monstrous greenhouse on wheels feel dizzy and disorientated.

FLAT TYRE RATING: 🛞🛞

Infiniti FX50
2009

GRATUITOUS UGLINESS never sits well with me, but this is the pits. The Infiniti FX50 looks like a fat person with a small head wearing lots of jewellery, and sits on colossal wheels with black rubber bands wrapped around them so the ride quality is truly terrible. Why would anyone ever buy one? What's that? Big discount? It could never be enough. This was one of the first cars with cameras everywhere, because it's impossible to judge the extremities otherwise. An inexcusable abomination.

FLAT TYRE RATING: 🛞🛞🛞🛞

Infiniti M35h
2011

A POSH Nissan gets all dressed up and does two things. First off, it changes its name to Infiniti, and secondly, it's a hell of a lot of kit for not a lot of cash. Where could Nissan go wrong? The Infiniti brand was a banker, a sure-fire money-maker. Except for one thing. Its cars were terrible and no amount of cost-cutting could persuade anyone with more than a pebble for a brain to part with a cent. Luckily, someone's since explained to Infiniti that the kind of people who want luxury vehicles don't shop at Woolworths, so instead of producing 'value for money' motors, it has now started making some half-decent cars. Shame, then, that the penny hadn't dropped before Nissan came up with the dangerously scary Infiniti M35h in 2011. This half-electric 1948kg (4300lb) tub of lard may have had the power of Mike Tyson, but it handled like a pickpocket wearing boxing gloves. Even in a straight line its back end would do a fair impression of a drunk on a mission, but in the wet it was so terrifying you only had to twiddle your toes and you could end up in a hedge, a brick wall or under a truck. Despite its size, the boot wasn't much use either. This car was so full of batteries that you'd look great turning up in it at the golf club, but a complete fool when your wife delivered your trolley and clubs in a following car.

FLAT TYRE RATING:

Inflamborghini Gallardo
2003-2013

THIS ISN'T here for its lack of performance, or handling, or charisma, or looks. It made the list because more Lamborghini Gallardos have spontaneously combusted than been wrecked by the sons of Taiwanese shrimp paste exporters. Attempting a 'burn-out' in one of these often results in exactly that. They smoulder, immolate, and turn to ash almost every week on 'Wrecked Exotics,' and this poses three questions: Why did Lamborghini design a car with an external combustion engine? Why would anyone want to drive a car with a potential bonfire behind them? And why didn't anyone think of fitting a fire extinguishing system to the car?

GEORGE ADDS: The one thing you couldn't fault the Gallardo for was its outrageous noise. I drove the lightweight Superleggera version, and although it turned the view into a scene like being in the cockpit of the Millennium Falcon in *Star Wars*, it sounded like a war. Later some friends of mine who'd been playing golf said: "Were you testing that Lamborghini on Saturday morning?" I confirmed I had been, and one said: "We thought so. We could hear it from five miles away." Think that's good? It also meant that cops could hear it coming from the moment you left home.

FLAT TYRE RATING: 🛞🛞🛞

KIA Carens
2000-2006

THE SAVING grace of the original KIA Carens was that it had one of the first sat nav systems that linked up to the free European traffic jam avoidance network. So, even 14 years ago, it would guide you around hold-ups. We went to visit my daughter in Leerdam, Holland, from which there were at least two routes to Calais via Belgium, and it saved us hours by telling us the most direct was blocked by a crash. Apart from that, it was the sort of MPV that if you offered to take your kids to school, they would politely ask you to park behind something so none of their schoolmates could see them getting out. And so its market became mostly Motability and the elderly who were more concerned about not having to bend to get in than about what they were getting into. Gradually the message from the public got listened to. We don't want MPVs that look like Special Needs vehicles. We want 'Crossovers'. Which is why the current KIA Carens doesn't sell in significant numbers, but the KIA Sportage does.

FLAT TYRE RATING:

KIA Rio
2001-2005

THIS 'VALUE for money' monster was like driving a dustbin. Ugly, nasty and cheap in every sense of the word. The press launch using 'The Bridge' from Copenhagen to Malmo failed to impress (no Saga Noren) and a relaunch of the Mk II involving 'La Discotoria,' a club in suburban Barcelona, turned into an all-night drinking session with the Italian contingent retiring to a girlie bar in Castelldefels, and dawn breaking over some severely sore heads. There is absolutely nothing good to say about this car at all. Even if it had been two grand, that would have been a grand too much. Happily, the 2nd generation KIA Rio was a good little car for sensible money (thanks to the then KIA UK MD, Paul Williams), and the present one out-styles the Fiesta.

FLAT TYRE RATING:
🛞🛞🛞🛞🛞

KIA Carnival/Sedona
1999-2006

ANOTHER CONFECTION from the long gone days when KIAs weren't much kop. Much loved by large, low-income families and airport taxi drivers – an affection not shared by me. Seats arranged 2-2-3, like a bus, and, in some parts of the world, an extra three were squeezed in. Gears were selected by a manual porridge-stirrer or a Dawldlematic torque-converter slushbox that dithered over every change of ratio. But the worst offence was terminal understeer from the terrible power steering. Acceptable in a straight line, but not on corners, where it tended to slither off the road if anything approaching grip was requested of the front tyres. Later, this was sorted out, and now there's a brand new one in other parts of the world, with up to four rows of seats, but the best place for the original is the jaws of a scrapyard crusher.

FLAT TYRE RATING:
⊗ ⊗ ⊗

72

CT 200h

Lexus CT 200h
2011

GOOD NEWS. The Lexus CT 200h has changed so much since it first appeared in 2011, that it now almost deserves that ultra-posh Lexus badge. Here's a car that proves manufacturers *do* listen to criticism, because back then they should have dusted off the old Corolla badge and given it that. Fair enough, it was mechanically superb, but Toyota's claim that it would "bring a new and younger customer to the Lexus brand" was totally absurd. The original CT200h was such a dull and boring motor that I doubt even the easiest to please pensioner would find it in any way interesting or exciting. The drive could best be described as bumbling; features like power and handling were never going to be tested by journalists or its owners, because they were completely irrelevant to the need to achieve a claimed average figure of 69mpg. The best I could manage, anyway, was 50mpg driven in a straight line on the flat trying not to touch the throttle. Far from being a 'Lexus,' the doors were finished in what appeared to be child-resistant hard plastic, and the executive passengers sitting in the rear seats of a

brand normally driven by chauffeurs would have to be children, such was the lack of legroom. Back then, it was terrible. New versions are far better, and may have arrived soon enough to banish the original from the memory banks.

FLAT TYRE RATING:

Maserati 3200 GT
1998-2002

WHAT TWO words could be more totally terrifying than Maserati 3200 GT? Well, okay, one word, four numbers and two letters, but if I'd started: "What one word, four numbers and two letters …" you get the picture. You'd have turned the page by now. No doubt about it, though, that just after taking over their Italian rivals, Ferrari's first effort at making a Maserati was about as scary as it gets. Appearances, as they say, can be deceiving, and the gorgeous looking 3200 GT, designed by Giorgetto Giugiaro's Italdesign company, and built in Modena (near Ferrari's home town of Maranello), was so beautiful to behold, you'd have found it hard to believe it was an angel with an AK-47. The 3200 GT's beautiful boomerang rear lights and gorgeous sculpted bonnet hid from sight its wild 3.2-litre V8 twin turbo with – considering it came out in 1998 – a brutal 372hp. If only life was that simple. Driving the 3200 GT, with its stuttering power delivery, was strange and quite often a let down. You'd floor it, wait for it to decide if was a nice day or not, then be hammered into the seatbacks as it took off like a cobra with a belly full of marbles. Controlling it was almost impossible, and the best way to describe its steering was "hanging on for grim death" as it took whatever direction it felt like. Now imagine the same experience in the wet. No, you can't. It was like playing table tennis in a hurricane. The best way to drive a 3200 GT was to simply cruise along and let people gawp at it. In the rain it had so little grip, you felt like it would slide off the road at a moment's notice. Braking, or putting your foot down, was a complete no-no, and you'd soon spot there was a queue of trucks behind you. If all that wasn't bad enough, the interior build quality was questionable to say the least. I discovered that when the roof lining collapsed over my head on a motorway.

HJ SAYS: I don't know what George is on about here. A friend of mine got an enjoyable five years out of one bought for £11k and sold at an Historics auction for £8k. I actually preferred the 3.2 twin-turbos to the later V8s. They seemed to get up to 160mph more quickly and felt more settled there. But maybe the Millbrook two-mile bowl had become bumpier by the time I drove the later car.

FLAT TYRE RATING: 🛞🛞🛞

Maserati Ghibli
2013

CROCKS OF crap don't get much bigger than the 2013 Maserati Ghibli, in every possible way. This enormous 16ft 4in out-of-control monster wasn't just massive, it was a massive letdown. At a starting price of fifty grand, rising to £63,000 for a top-spec car which was almost as hugely equipped as it was disappointing, it proved an equally huge waste of cash. Let's start with the good news, though. It looked and sounded fantastic, like a proper snarling yet beautiful beast that would eat up anything stupid enough to get in its way. Oh, and then there's … there's … no, there's nothing. Absolutely nothing else you could find that was even remotely good about it. The crackling noise from its 330hp 3.0-litre V6's four cavern-like exhausts was enough to wake your distant neighbours, but it was quickly drowned out the first time you tried to park it by the painful wrenching sound of the front tyres being torn from their rims. To make matters worse, it juddered and bounced about on top of them as they nearly collapsed under its ponderous weight. Then there was its road holding, or lack of. On anything but a perfect surface its rear-wheel-drive setup felt like it could easily spin around in a full 360-degree circle just by twiddling your toes. It was so fidgety it was like a teenager on a first date. It may have been mightily quick, with 0-62mph in 5.8 seconds, but trying to drive it in a straight line was nigh-on impossible, as it followed every deviation in the road surface, however small. You didn't dare floor it, because the back wheels scrabbled for grip as the whole car snaked from side to side, while the steering was so uncontrollable it did a good imitation of belonging to a different car. The fear of flying off the side of the road into a hedge, or, worse still, a tree, was intensified by the terror of it veering into the other side of the road in front of an oncoming truck. Seriously, any tiny bump could have caused this. Could it get worse? Oh yes it could. Trying to find reverse was almost as impossible as getting a successful result on a motorway service station game that uses a mini crane to pick up something as fabulous as a three quid watch. I had it for a week, during which I prayed that someone would nick it. Trouble is, you'd have to be a pretty stupid crook who knew totally nothing about cars to imagine it would be worth stealing.

FLAT TYRE RATING: 🛞🛞🛞🛞

Maybach 62
2005-2014

SUPPOSED TO be the autobahnstorming symbol of success for German business-men, Far Eastern inheritors of sultanates and African dictators, the Maybach was a bigger, glitzier Mercedes-Benz S Class, without the class. *Dragon's Den*'s Theo Paphitis took his a step further by having it wrapped in mirrorplate, so when it was parked outside Café One in Weybridge he could watch himself having breakfast with Max Clifford, Peter Crouch, Abbey Clancy, and Adam Crozier (not necessarily all at the same time, and no longer with Max Clifford). There's discrete good taste, there's-in-your face wealth, and there's gold-plated everything.

FLAT TYRE RATING:

81

Mazda Demio
1998-2002

IF YOU thought the Mazda Premacy was a pile of poo when it first soiled the streets, Mazda managed to come up with an even uglier surprise in 1998, in the form of so-called 'Toyota Yaris rival,' the Demio. At least, I think that's how you spell it because it should have been Dummio. This car was so dire it must have taken its inspiration from a takeaway kebab shop at 4am on a Sunday morning. Just looking at its lifeless, unimaginative, corpse of a body was enough to make you sick, but opening its doors and getting in should have been more than enough to complete the job. Inside, it was a world of flat, dull, black and grey plastic, and thoughtlessly scattered-about boring black and white dials that were, unbelievably, only beaten to a Treadmill Trophy by its lifeless 1.3-litre 53hp engine and snail-like progress. It wasn't just painfully slow, it was gutless. A competitor to the Yaris? More like a brilliant Yaris promotion poster. Goodbye for ever couldn't come soon enough, and thankfully it did in 2002 when it was replaced by the Ford Fusion-based, 2nd generation Demio-badged Mazda 2 in Europe.

FLAT TYRE RATING:

Mercedes-Benz CLK Convertible
1999-2002

ON THE face of it there's not a lot to dislike about the soft top version of the CLK. Fair enough, the original 200CLK was desperately slow and needed the engine update it later got, but it was well-equipped and, when it was launched, its ingenious electric folding roof brought it plenty of adoring attention. I was happy to show it off when I got to my local petrol station to fill it up before a 350-mile round trip to drive the first ever Jaguar E-type, which had just been restored to its former glory. The Jaguar proved to be even more rewarding that I'd dared dream. The drive home in the Merc was one of the most annoying and painful experiences I'd ever suffered in a car, especially a Mercedes. For starters, it was so cramped it felt like I was in a giant straitjacket. Getting even remotely comfortable was completely impossible, and I kept having to stop to stretch my legs. If I'd had any passengers, especially in the rear, they'd have topped themselves if they could have reached into their pockets, which, of course, they couldn't. In the dark the instruments were so badly lit they may as well have been invisible, and, as I was either boiling hot or freezing to death, adjusting the temperature was impossible. Headroom was so low that even little me got cramp in my neck and rear view vision was non-existent, making pulling out a game of Russian roulette. Getting home had never been so enjoyable, but the trip had been totally unforgettable. Thank you, the Jaguar E-type.

HJ ADDS: Back in 1999, I was doing a TV show called *Dealer's Choice*, that was a sort of *Changing Rooms* but about cars. A couple would pick a car and I, or one of half a dozen other 'dealers,' would attempt to persuade them to choose something else. The guy who got most of the cars for us was Tom Hardiment of Paradise Garage, who'd just taken delivery of a brand new CLK 320 convertible himself, only to discover to his chagrin that it was already falling apart.

FLAT TYRE RATING: ⚙ ⚙ ⚙ ⚙

Mercedes-Benz W210 E-Class
1995-2002

THIS IS in because no car epitomises Mercedes-Benz' catastrophic drop in quality as effectively as the W210 Mercedes-Benz E-Class. After some idiot decided to save money on Mercedes bodywork pre-paint treatment, all Mercedes from 1997 to 2003 rusted badly, especially in the seams. But on the W210 the front suspension spring perches corroded so comprehensively that it became common to see W210s slammed to the ground at the front without any attention from *Fast n' Loud*'s Aaron Kaufman. Surprisingly, VOSA refused to issue a vehicle safety recall over this issue. (I had correspondence with a Mr Sweeting of VOSA.) If the cars were serviced properly by Mercedes-Benz dealers they were supposed to be covered by a 30-year Mobilo no rust-through warranty, but interpretation of that warranty left a lot of owners with empty pockets and a bad taste in the mouth. Somehow, Mercedes seemed to get away with an eight-year limit on the no rust-through warranty and, since by eight years old, most of these cars were being serviced by Tom, Dick or Harry at the local independent, they didn't qualify for Mobilo anyway.

FLAT TYRE RATING:

Mercedes-Benz A-Class
1998-2005

SOMEONE IN the accounts department at Mercedes-Benz told the management it was losing a fortune by engineering its cars like no other in the world. So when Mercedes made its first small car, its designers bore this warning in mind. The A-Class was almost stillborn because by 1998 cars were required to dodge their way past any Elks that happened to wander into the road, and when this was attempted in the all-new mini-Mercedes the car fell over. Of course, Mercedes fixed that, sort of, and on the press launch we all had to avoid simulated Elks. But cost-engineering still meant that on the RHD A-Class the steering wheel was on one side of the car, and its entry point to the steering rack was on the other, with a long bar and some CV joints in between. Dare to sneeze on the motorway and you were in serious trouble. The sandwich construction of the floor that was supposed to send the engine under your feet in a head-on crash also meant that it was impossible for a mechanic to access, so to do any work on it he had to take it out. After about six years, owners of six-year old A-Class were facing £6000 bills to fix simple things like clutches and gearboxes, and A-Classes were finding their way to where they always really belonged. The scrapheap.

FLAT TYRE RATING:

Mercedes-Benz R-Class
2006-2013

PEOPLE NATURALLY think that Mercedes-Benz cars are German. But they aren't *all* German. In 1993, Mercedes announced it would build a factory in Vance, Alabama (near Tuscaloosa), and its first ML model emerged from the production line there in 1997, the same year that Mercedes-Benz quality worldwide took a dive off a cliff. The ML was fault-ridden from day one, and was hideously ugly with an optional spare wheel suspended on what looked like scaffolding at the back. But the ML wasn't enough to keep the good ole boys working at peak inefficiency. For that, Mercedes-Benz of America created the R-Class, a 17-foot, four-wheel drive, six-seater leviathan. Most that found their way to the UK had MB's 3.0-litre V6 320CDI diesel engine but, with an all-up weight of 2270kg without any Americans inside, even that had trouble hauling along this colossal car, and didn't leave much for a caravan. The biggest surprise – apart from feeling dwarfed by the thing – was the handling. The similar length Mercedes S-Class was always decent to drive, but this lump of lard had serious trouble making any change of direction. All the more peculiar because the full-fat SUV version, called the GL, which stood more than a foot taller, and was made in the same factory, was actually a jolly decent old bus that I could happily drive 1000 miles in a day, as long as it didn't break down.

FLAT TYRE RATING:

MG Rover CityRover
2003-2005

IT COULD hardly be coincidence that the appalling CityRover was built by the same company that made my worst car of all time. That firm was, of course, Tata, which was responsible for the unbelievably awful Tata Safari. Made in India and marketed under the name Tata Indica, the CityRover brought new levels of industrial inefficiency to unsuspecting grandmothers who put their faith in the dying Rover badge. If you tried out one and still bought it you'd have been totally mad. It was a catalogue of disasters that seemed to offer a new problem every day, starting with the moment you got in it, to discover that the seats were ridiculously high and offered no escape route by being adjustable. Worse still, the steering wheel couldn't be adjusted, either. Once driven, the CityRover was never to be forgotten. Its 1.4-litre motor was so noisy it sounded like something had come loose inside, and its ride, regardless of road surface, was unacceptably bouncy, and just added to the racket coming from the engine compartment. All the time it was begging for a well-balanced gearbox, but instead you had to keep trying to keep the revs down, or change gear to keep it going. Driving around bends was terrifying. You turned the steering wheel but nothing happened. It didn't seem to be in any way connected to the wheels, while the wheels themselves didn't seem to be bolted to the chassis. The whole car just collapsed as it fell away, leaving the driver hanging on to the steering wheel and praying that it would get around something as tough as a gentle bend. Changing gear was like fishing in the dark with a lump hammer, and at times you expected its spindly gearlever to snap off. In the wind and rain the wipers blew away so much they actually failed to make contact with the windscreen. Neither the fiddly radio, the stupidly small boot, or the tiny glovebox had lights, so were useless in the dark. It was ridiculously thirsty, but the fuel gauge read full on left-hand bends and empty on right-handers. The low petrol warning light stayed on permanently after its first of many fill-ups, as did the dashboard light to tell you that a door was open. A buzzer was supposed to tell you if you'd left the headlights switched on. The only buzz I heard was my doorbell when a neighbour came round at night to tell me that the lights were still on. The fresh air vents couldn't be switched off and only blew cold, the seat belts were charmingly positioned so they cut right across your neck, and the vanity mirror in the passenger sunvisor had a black cover which fell on top of it if you wanted to use it. The switches were set in a wobbly, ill-fitting plastic box to the right of the steering wheel, and all this in the car that MG Rover lent to me: a top spec 'Style' version ...

HJ COMMENTS: I first saw the Tata Indica (probably along with George) at the 1999 Barcelona Motor Show, which was always the most enjoyable motor show on the calendar (the tapas came out at 11.00am). The Indica looked fine by the standards of the day. Its disaster lay in Rover's attempt to re-launch it in the UK in 2003 at premium prices, in a duplicitous attempt to 'save Rover' by flogging an Indian car on which the only Rover bits were the badges. Apparently, MG Rover paid Tata £3000 a car, including import duties and VAT, then attempted to sell them on at prices from £6500 to £8500. A few patriotic folk were fooled, but ended up smiling

2004 Rover CityRover, photo copyright Tom Ellis, from Wikimedia.

smugly when, ten years later, they found the cars had proved to be impressively reliable. The exercise had also shown Tata how to make a decent margin on a car, which it then put into practice much more effectively with Jaguar Land Rover.

FLAT TYRE RATING: 🛞🛞🛞🛞🛞

MINI Countryman
2011

THIS OVERGROWN MINI actually comes from Austria, and looks like it's been fed too many strudels. Yet you can't blame MINI marketing, because it's actually the best selling 'MINI' in the world. However, I do feel entitled to criticise the car. There are lots of different versions: manuals and automatics; petrols and diesels; two-wheel drives and four-wheel drives, and it's possible to spend thirty grand on one. Why, isn't abundantly clear. The standard two-wheel drive versions drive as blandly as Toyota Corollas did 15 years ago. There is literally no fun to be had at all. Push one into a corner and it goes so squodgy you decide never to do that again. With four-wheel drive it livens up a bit, and might get you through a few inches of snow or a grassy field. But lots of better cars, like the Golf AllTrack, SEAT Leon X-perience, Skoda Octavia Scout, Skoda Yeti, and Suzuki Vitara, do it much better. So why housewives across the globe demand that their salarymen supply them with a Countryman is proof (if proof ever were needed) that people will buy anything if it is marketed at them right (or maybe they thought a Countryman was a substitute husband for the daytime).

FLAT TYRE RATING: 🛞🛞

Mitsubishi Carisma
1995-2004

CARMAKERS COME up with some great names ... Viper, Scorpio, Mondeo, Astra and, of course, Beetle. They all tell us something about the car, and some names are truly legendary. So when Mitsubishi came up with the Carisma it must have been delighted. Fact was, it couldn't have come up with a worse name to describe one of the most boring cars imaginable. Yes, the Carisma did everything you could want from a motor in a perfectly efficient way, but it was so *dull*, so *lifeless*, so *dreary* that a better name for it would have been the Mitsubishi Apathy. And it wasn't just its dreadful suspension, underpowered engine and banal looks that made it such a dud. Add to that seats that were impossible to live with for more than 15 minutes and an auto box that was as vague as a pub drunk, and it all adds up to a catastrophe of immense proportions. By the time Mitsubishi realised that it wasn't selling, things had gone too far. It slashed the price, beefed up the engine and suspension, added stacks of kit as standard, and turned the Carisma into something of a bargain. Shame it hadn't thought of that earlier. By then the damage had been done and the car withered away like a weed in winter.

HJ ADDS: Born alongside the Mitsubishi Carisma at Volvo's old factory in Born, Holland (where the Volvo 340 was also born) were the 'posh' versions, dubbed Volvo S40 and Volvo V40. Handling was vague at the best of times, but the one delivered to me to test for a week wouldn't steer at all. Somehow I managed to conduct it to the local Volvo dealer who had never seen one before, yet still ascertained it had so much toe-in it was virtually knock-kneed. It still drove like a diver with nitrogen in his bloodstream (it had a fit of the bends) but did at least reply to the steering wheel, though refused to answer it directly. Like the Carisma, some of the engines fitted were an early development of petrol direct injection and led to the discovery that, unless run exclusively on superfuels, the system cokes up its inlet valves.

FLAT TYRE RATING: 🛞 🛞 🛞

CARISMA

Mitsubishi i-MIEV
2011

THE i-MIEV was an early attempt to electrify a £5000 Japanese lightweight 'Kei Car' and was also badge-engineered by Peugeot and Citroën. For a tiddler, it was actually quite good fun to drive, and would even pull 80mph if asked to. But, due to the cost of the battery, it was a tiny tin box at an eyewatering price. Even after a £5000 government grant, it wanted £33,699. Realising that was nuts, Peugeot offered its iON-badged version at an all-inclusive £498 a month, at which point company car guru Simon Harris got out his calculator and soon figured that the only people who would lease one would be corporations and companies that wanted to pretend to be green. Citroën failed to sell more than a handful of its i-MIEV badged C-Zeros at £26,995 so reduced the price to £16,995, and, at the time of writing, was still stuck with them.

FLAT TYRE RATING:

Mitsuoka Viewt Mk II
1993-2010

ORIGINALLY BASED on the K11 'Mr Blobby' March/Micra, this looked like a kiddie car that had been designed by children to create a conveyance for four of them, with the appearance of a Mk II Jaguar. They failed. (They were just kids, after all.) Real stylists like Jaguar's Ian Callum and custom car creator Rick Dore have an eye for what looks exactly right. They stand back and check and make minor alterations until the shape is perfect. This lot needed a visit to Specsavers. Underneath the Viewt's ill-proportioned body lay the perfectly reasonable mechanicals of a K11 March/Micra 1.3, including a manual or CVT transmission. Then, from 2005 there was a similarly ghastly K12-based version. Sold by dealers with laughing stock.

FLAT TYRE RATING:

Mitsuoka Galue II
2009-2005

I FIRST clapped eyes on this coachbuilding catastrophe in concept form at the Bangkok Motor Show of March 2008, where the glamour has been known to distract attention from the disasters on display. Based on the oddly-named Nissan Cedric and powered by 2.5- or 3.0-litre V6s, it was supposed to provide limousine luxury to visually impaired Japanese businessmen with no taste. The Americans once tried and failed to do something similar with a monstrosity called the Excalibur. For them, Mitsuoka rebodied a 1997 Ford Mustang 4.6 to create the Galue convertible. Even Merlin the Magician couldn't do much to help its sales figures.

FLAT TYRE RATING:
🛞🛞🛞🛞🛞

Morgan Plus 8
1972

NOSTALGIA GONE nuts. Great retro looks, but sliding pillar front suspension that dates back 100 years. Crippling driving position. Backbreaking ride, unless you deflate the pneumatic seat cushions. And you have to call in Rentokil every few years to get rid of the termites in the wood frame body. Masochistic endurance enthusiasts adore them, because the experience brings back memories of fagging at public school and the abject misery of cross-country runs in the rain. So very English. One of the best advertising copywriters ever to have lived (Tony Brignull) once made the mistake, and afterwards described it as "The sort of car for people who wear bobble hats and have oil under their fingernails."

FLAT TYRE RATING: 🛞

Nissan Figaro
1990-1991

NISSAN'S ODDLY-NAMED 'Pike' vehicle factory (actually the Aichi Machine Industry plant) turned out a series of whacky one-offs in the 1990s, designed by Naoki Sakai. There was the Be-1; the S-Cargo, a small van that looked like a snail; the Pao, a sort of jungle utility car, and 12,000 Figaros, for which demand was so high that cars were allocated by lottery in a choice of Topaz Mist, Emerald Green, Pale Aqua and Lapis Grey. All had a white plastic steering wheel, an electric canvas sunroof and retro wheeltrims. They look great (if you like that sort of thing), a bit like a 1950s Goggomobile, but were based on the 1.0-litre belt cam K10 Micra, fitted with a turbocharger and a three-speed automatic transmission that hardly turned them into balls of fire. Like K10 Micras, they are also extremely rust-prone, particularly in the rear wings.

FLAT TYRE RATING: 🛞🛞

Nissan Serena diesel
1993-2000

JUST AS the inappropriately-named Mitsubishi Carisma had none, the Nissan Serena diesel was anything but. It drove with the same resistance to forward motion as a 1946 London bus, struggling in a series of unpleasant jerks through five manual gears to a maximum speed of something like 56mph. Though offered with various other engines and even four wheel drive, redemption never came its way. You may occasionally see one in a Spanish scrapyard, forlornly waiting to be cannibalised for parts by an owner who never comes because the ocular disorder that led him to buy his Serena in the first place caused him to drive onto an unmanned level crossing in front of a train.

FLAT TYRE RATING: ⚙ ⚙ ⚙ ⚙ ⚙

Nissan Almera
1995-2006

WHEN THE first generation Nissan Almera reached the UK back in 1995 I immediately set about slaughtering it. No, not because it was built in Japan, I couldn't care less where a car comes from, but because it was a truly detestable little effort. Plasticky and noisy with a pitiful performance, a lousy ride, and just enough space for mum's kids and her shopping, it was one to avoid, and well worth the effort too. Trouble is, it was practical and cheap, so it sold so well that the ghastly things were everywhere. That's why, instead of making them in Oppama and shipping them over to Europe, Nissan decided to transfer production to their giant car plant in Sunderland in 2000, and three years later a face-lifted version rolled off the production line. It was still great value, with lots of kit that you wouldn't have expected fitted as standard, such as electric windows, remote locking, a CD player and, a real luxury touch, air-conditioning. That, for customers, was the good news. Sadly, nothing else had changed. Cheap materials and a poor build quality were still abundantly obvious. The seats made my bottom ache, the plastic fittings rattled, the handbrake and steering wheel were thin and nasty, like something from the Seventies, and once you dared go over 70mph the wind noise made it whistle like a kettle, making it extremely unpleasant. This car for mums didn't do handling. It didn't need to. It was nasty, but cheap and practical, which were the two only reasons it lasted until 2006, when Nissan finally shot it. Dead.

FLAT TYRE RATING: 🛞🛞

Perodua Kancil/Nippa
1997-2002

A TINY tin box made in Malaysia and based on a deceased Daihatsu. Known as the Perodua Kancil in Malaysia, it was renamed for the UK in case buyers kancilled their orders. A victim of the collapse of the Far Eastern Tiger economies in 1997, they became the cheapest cars dumped in the UK, priced from £4495 with a two-year warranty. Under the bonnet if you searched hard and it wasn't dark, you'd find a tiny 660cc engine with all of 31hp, or a more perky 37hp three-cylinder 850. Dangerously vulnerable on the motorway, and, when we hired one in Langkawi, we had to wait until the rain stopped for fear of the car floating away. The Kancil/Nippa was succeeded by the Perodua Kelisa, that lasted from 2002 to 2009. The saving graces of this Malaysian mishmash were a price of £4699 delivered, including a radio, and a width of just 1490mm (4' 11"), so even if your house had been designed by a penny-pinching developer you could get it into the garage, then get out of it. The car wasn't as bad as Clarkson's *Top Gear* crew led the world to believe, and was actually quite good fun to drive if you couldn't afford anything better. In 2006 CAP showed that it would lose less cash over three years than any other car.

GEORGE SAYS: I loved this little car. It had something called character, especially as it flew around bends, cruised well on the motorway and felt like a half-decent motorbike. It was only after handing it back to Perodua that I realised I'd had it for a week, during which time I hadn't gone over 45mph. There was good reason for that. It was too scary.

FLAT TYRE RATING: 🛞🛞🛞

Peugeot 407
2004-2011

THE CAR that replaced the immaculately-styled, long-lasting Peugeot 406, beloved by taxi drivers who could get 400,000 miles out of them. The gormless gob of the 407 had so much front overhang you could knock a wall down just manoeuvring out of your driveway (I know a man who did). The back seat was so claustrophobic, it was like travelling in a coal mine. As well as that, like other Peugeots of the day, it was very 'front-endy,' loading the front wheels and tyres for the pleasure of enthusiasts and the glee of dealers who made a fortune replacing suspension bushes.

FLAT TYRE RATING: 🛞🛞

Peugeot 1007
2005-2008

GOOD IDEAS don't always result in cars that sell, and if you ever need proof of this, try recalling the Peugeot 1007. Can't remember it? Never seen one? That's because Peugeot dropped it from the UK after just four years of sales in the hundreds rather than thousands, and a year later in the rest of Europe. Does it deserve its place in our Crocks of Crud? That's a difficult one, because, purely as a car, the 1007 was fine. In its day it was extremely fuel-efficient, well kitted out with some trendy modern gear, delightful to be in and good to drive. Well, if you don't count 0-60mph in 17 seconds and a 99mph top speed. And that pitiful lack of speed explains exactly why it was such a failure. You see, Peugeot expected it to be driven by young mums who don't give a damn how slow their car is as long as their beloved babies are safe. As one hysterical mum often screams in *The Simpsons*: "Will someone think of the children? For God's sake will someone please think of the children?" And that's where Peugeot went wrong. No one thought of the children, just their mothers. So what did Peugeot do to make life easier for mummy? It fitted the 1007 with huge electric sliding doors that were supposed to stop the moment someone touched them. Well, they didn't stop. In fact, they were so strong they would probably have floored a teenager, never mind a child. My five-year-old tester hadn't a hope in hell of stopping one going backwards. Blimey, it nearly knocked me over. There wasn't a mum in the world who would let her toddler go anywhere near a 1007. Imagine their thoughts as their child sat behind them, out of sight, playing with a door that could have sliced off their fingers, or worse, suddenly opened while the car was doing 50mph. Sorry, Peugeot, but the 1007 could have been a nice idea, if only someone had properly thought it through.

HJ SAYS: When Peugeot put this Citroën C2-based contraption up as a concept on its stand at the Paris Motor Show, the public said they loved its twin electric sliding doors. So Peugeot happily put it into production and hardly anyone bought it. Moral of the story: when people are researched with direct questions they often lie. To get the truth you have to use trick questions. **FLAT TYRE RATING:** 🛞🛞🛞

Pontiac Aztek
2001-2005

CANCER-SUFFERING CHEMISTRY teacher Walter White's car in *Breaking Bad*, deliberately chosen because it epitomised life's wrong choices, failures, frustrations, and a total lack of taste. Conceived as an all-purpose, practical 'sport recreational vehicle,' capable of carrying 8' x 4' sheets of plywood, and offered with camping accessories for lifestyle adventures in the great outdoors, it was put to good use when Walter got down to a bit of DIY replacing the boiler in his house (that's the heating boiler, not the other one). The windscreen of Walt's Aztek got smashed several times, most memorably by debris when deceased stoner Jayne's grieving air-traffic controller dad directed a couple of planes into each other after she overdosed. It was effectively America's Austin Maxi, but worse-looking and better built.

FLAT TYRE RATING:

Renault Mégane
1996-2001

RENAULTS ARE a lot better now than they used to be; actually more reliable than Volkswagens or Fords, according to reports from my readers. But back in the 1990s they were so bad I resorted to renaming then 'Renfaults.' Imagine taking delivery of a test car for a week (a petrol-engined Mégane 1.6) and immediately finding that it won't start. Renault sent out a 'tech,' who quickly diagnosed a failed flywheel sensor. That got fixed, but it didn't prevent the complaints from flooding in, and not just to me. In June 2001 Renault was rated by Warranty Direct as Britain's joint 4th worst out of 22 marques for used car warranty claims, and was fifth bottom in the 2002 *Which?* reliability survey of 184 models up to two years old. It even caused a minor international incident. There I was, soaking up some equatorial sun on the beach at Bali, when a South African lady who was married to a French diplomat discovered what I did, and decided to ask me about her husband's car. You know what's coming. I desperately tried to avoid answering, but eventually she forced it out of me and later informed the monsieur. Had I told him his wife was the skankiest old slapper I had ever seen it would have had a less volcanic effect. I had not only offended him, I had trampled the French flag into the sand, and been responsible for a more reprehensible outrage than inventing 'Boeuf Wellington.' The entente could not have been less cordiale. However, the Mégane did at least respond to the steering wheel quite decently, so only three 'FLAT TYRES.'

FLAT TYRE RATING:

Renault Avantime
2001-2003

BORN IN 2001, dead and buried by 2003. That was the short-lived mega-disaster that was the horrific Renault Avantime. Its name was supposed to mean 'before it's time.' Well I'm sorry, but it may as well have meant 'before we thought about it.' The catastrophe got under way the night before the launch around Berlin, when Renault sent a garage load of 'I really haven't had time' motors to the hotel, to take us to a barge on the River Spree for a pre-drive party. We got in the car two at a time, in the back. We got out 15 minutes later almost unable to walk. Despite its size, this massive motor was so cramped in the back they should have invited a party of junior school kids to review it. Next day, driving it around what seemed like the whole of Germany, was one of the most tedious days of my life. We endured every pothole and bump in the country as we lurched around from village to village for seven ghastly hours. At least the driver could hang on to the steering wheel, as the front seat passenger continually slid off and nearly vanished inside the footwell. The seat sloped downwards at the front and wasn't adjustable. Every time we stopped to stretch our shattered bodies, we had to find somewhere wide enough to open its giant three and a half feet wide doors, with no window frames or door pillars, which just added to the feeling of being thrown around in an extremely uncomfortable tin can. They say that people will buy anything, provided it looks cool. Well that's obviously a load of old rubbish. Buyers voted with their chequebooks, by refusing to open them.

HJ ADDS: Needless to say the hinges on those metre-long doors didn't hang on for long, and door droop was the most common complaint. But George must have liked the big Renaults of the day. He put his dad into the Vel Satis, that was like an IKEA living room-sized version of the Avantime with four more sensible side-doors.

FLAT TYRE RATING: 🛞🛞🛞🛞🛞

Renault Twingo GT
2007-2014

IF THE Renault Twingo was a film it would be called 'The Good, The Bad and The Pretty.' It was very nearly a half-decent motor but its bad sides catapult it into our Saga of Shame. Let's start, though, with its good points. Here was a sweet looking motor that vaguely reminded you of the original and ultra-desirable Twingo. Sweet, but not quite sweet enough. Then there was its engine. It may only have been a 1.2, but bang on a turbo and it was good for nearly 120mph and 0-62mph in under 10 seconds. Shame then, that as well as offering near 50mpg fuel consumption, it was noisy and never stopped whining about how hard it was working. Aah, but its interior was clever and smart, with adjustable rear seats, lots of storage spaces and plenty of up-to-date kit. Add that to a sub £10,000 price tag and it might just have been acceptable. But that's before you consider it didn't have the sixth gear it was begging for, the way it snaked and veered from side to side on take-off, with its front wheels scrabbling for grip like a lamb on a crumbling cliff top, the constant stalling at low speed, its bouncy ride and its weird instruments that made it look like someone actually tried, but nowhere near hard enough.

HJ ADDS: The feature that made sense with the second generation Twingo was its pair of separately-sliding rear seats. These meant that even in a car 3600mm long you could have decent rear legroom, providing, of course, there were no eggs in the supermarket bag you'd put behind the rear seats ...

FLAT TYRE RATING: 🛞🛞

Renault Fluence ZE
2012-2014

THE RENAULT Fluence ZE was designed at a time when Renault was planning battery exchange service stations for electric cars. The idea was, you hummed into a service station and drove over a contraption that removed your old battery from beneath and replaced it with a new, freshly charged one. That's why, though the Fluence ZE is quite a big car, it doesn't offer outstanding rear legroom, or a particularly big boot, because there's a removable battery the size of a dead body in between. In its favour, the Fluence ZE makes quite a smooth, quick city taxi as long as the charge in the battery holds out. It just doesn't look right, and in the UK it didn't sell until they offered it at a 50% discount, and electric enthusiasts, who will regale you for hours about their zero tailpipe emissions and low running costs, rushed in to buy it. I don't think many of them live within the environs of Ferrybridge or Kegworth coal-fired power stations.

GEORGE SAYS: Not surprisingly, this feeble French failure was quickly nicknamed the Renault Flatulence by clever clogs British hacks who thought they were way above driving such a vehicle. I never stepped into one either, because with a name like that it must have been a right stinker.

FLAT TYRE RATING:

SAAB 900 and 9-3
1993-2002

THE FIRST incarnation of GM's smothering of SAAB. Basically a Cavalier, complete with steering rack screwed to a weak bulkhead and SAAB mechanicals. The SAAB bits worked, the GM bits didn't, and, with a turbo attached, the front wheels would spin without the car going anywhere and the steering rack would detach itself. It could also be had with one of the first incarnations of a robotised automated manual transmission that didn't work, and should have been a lesson for others not to even try such nonsense. A lesson that automaker's accountants seeking short-term economies ignored, before making a career move and leaving their replacements to pick up the pieces.

FLAT TYRE RATING:
🛞🛞🛞

SEAT Marbella
1988-1995

THIS UNGLAMOROUS horror-show on wheels was the last incarnation of the original FIAT/SEAT Panda, still sitting on a simple rear axle with single leaf springs, powered by a puny 903cc pushrod engine, robbed of any character by a Frankenstein face-lift, and sometimes painted pink. Unlikely ever to be seen in Puerto Banus, where such basic transport is confined to underground car parks or dusty compounds on the edge of town, and only tolerated there because how else could they ship in the people who clean the toilets? Sincerely, the worst thing SEAT ever did, and whoever thought they could successfully restyle the definitively rustic Giugiaro original anyway?

FLAT TYRE RATING: 🛞 🛞 🛞 🛞

SEAT Toledo
2005-2009

NO, NOT the perfectly decent previous two generations of Toledo that starred in the BBC's ill-fated *Eldorado* ex-pat soap. This is the elephantine-assed bastard child of Walter d'Silva's reign as head of styling at SEAT. How could the man who designed the exquisite Alfa Romeo 156 ever have brought us this bloated barge of a Barcelona taxicab? I guess there must have been a 'marketing' requirement for luggage lugging that wasn't met by the SEAT Leon, even though it was by the SEAT Altea. 500 litres of baggage could be bunged in the boot – the one and only reason for the car.

FLAT TYRE RATING: 🛞🛞🛞

SEAT Ibiza Cupra Bocanegra
2010

SEAT CALLED in the local school when it got someone to design the Bocanegra. Trouble is, as much as the kids tried to wreck it, SEAT finished off the job for them. In spectacular style, too. The teens thought it would be great if the Bocanegra had the lot, by which I mean every child's fantasy of something that sounds and looks great. That's why they gave it a turbo and a supercharger, massive alloys with wafer-thin low profiles, smoked lights, a huge exhaust, a spoiler kit, a diffuser, sports suspension, racing seats, and a paddle shift gearbox. The lot cost twenty quid from Halfords, but the teens were delighted. Mrs Motormouth thought the local kids had parked one of their tarted-up old wrecks outside the house. Of course, none of these dreadful gimmicks actually worked. Its overworked 1.4-litre engine was nowhere near up to the job of making it seriously fast, and sounded like it was in terrible pain when pushed hard. The Bocanegra's stiff sports suspension threatened to break your back if you so much as drove over a McDonalds wrapper chucked away by its child-like designers, while its stupid wheels and tyres added to the general unpleasantness, shuddering and banging like crazy on anything other than a bowling alley-like surface. The word 'disaster' springs to mind, but, in reality, it was worse than that.

HJ ADDS: The disastrous 1.4TSI 'Twincharger' (German 'engine of the year') in Ibiza, Polo and Fabia vRS models (as well as in some Golfs and Alhambras) has been failing so badly that VAG has been forced to buy back some of the cars.

FLAT TYRE RATING: 🛞 🛞

Smart ForTwo
2000

IF YOU really, really, must buy a Smart car there are two things I beg of you. Firstly, make sure it's a model with Smart's new six-speed double-clutch gearbox, which, in early 2015, replaced the ghastly, impossible, five-speed contraption that had made all Smarts absolute cows to drive since they first popped through the letterbox back in 2000. Yep, the Smart ForTwo really is *that* small, but don't fall for the adverts that show girls with smiling faces, when in fact they should be throwing their handbags around in sheer frustration at not being able to change gear. Mind you, as if that wasn't bad enough Smart made things worse, considerably worse, by producing a diesel version in 2009. Here was a car that was so deafeningly noisy and bouncy it made the prospect of going to work in a tumble dryer seem more attractive. Lurching along the road from one neck-snapping gearchange to another, in a car that handled rough surfaces with all the finesse of a storm-tossed boat with a broken engine, was not something to look forward to. That's why it smelled when Smart took it home. My daughter was sick in it.

HJ ADDS: I can understand making a two-seater car as short as possible, and as safe as possible in a crash. But why did the third generation Smart ForTwo have to be so pointlessly, ridiculously ugly? In its favour is the fact that Smart finally gave up with its lurch-inducing, counter-intuitive automated manual transmission that made driving the first and second generation Smarts such misery. This one comes with a five-speed manual or a Renault-developed twin-shaft 'Efficient Dual Clutch' for those disinclined to use the stick. Smarts always made more sense in cities like Milan and Rome where the Truncated ForTwo is at least parkable. Unfortunately, trying some of the stunts they get away with there still earns you a ticket in Britain's city centres where the only culture is penalty culture.

FLAT TYRE RATING:

SSangYong Rodius
2005-2013

OBVIOUS, REALLY. But no list of knackers would be complete without the odious Rodius that could be forgiven if it had been styled by a myopic Korean, but it wasn't. It was styled by a bespectacled Brit. We can only assume that it originally looked okay, then the first committee made some changes, then the second committee put its oar in, then the chairman's wife (or mistress) submitted her ideas for the front and the world ended up with this ocular insult.

FLAT TYRE RATING:

Subaru Tribeca
2006-2010

I FELT genuinely sorry for Subaru during the launch of the terrible Tribeca, which was held in Venice in 2006. You couldn't fault its organisation: a terrific canal-front hotel, a stroll around one of the world's most famous cities, a fabulous dinner and, the next morning, an exciting, speed-filled, hour-long race to the roads just outside Venice in a gorgeous, varnished-wood 1940s Riva speedboat. I felt like James Bond. The rest of the launch, however, the bit we'd actually come for, can only be described as desperately dull, boring, and a complete waste of time for people who'd expected even a half-decent car, never mind an excellent one. The Tribeca, which was almost as big as the up-market New York district it was named after, weighed in at a proper heavyweight 1920kg – that's 4224lb. For power it had a 244hp, 3-litre Subaru Legacy Boxer engine, with a torque figure so puny, at 297Nm, it could barely drag itself around. Once we got it out into the country it comprehensively proved that its roly-poly ride hadn't been imagined, because Subaru had used bed springs and a bicycle pump for suspension, and the hazy steering seemed to be connected to the wheels by thought transference only. That's why it cornered like an ocean liner in a tropical storm. Subaru had another go at it in 2008 but dropped it in 2014, with total sales of just 78,000 cars, making it one of the worst-selling vehicles of all time.

FLAT TYRE RATING: 🛞🛞🛞🛞

Suzuki Katana Hi-Top
1997

THANKFULLY, THIS malevolent little monster was never sold in the UK. If you can imagine a Suzuki Jimny fitted with a high top, two-wheel-drive, an asthmatic 1-litre four-cylinder engine, and ridiculously wide aftermarket wheels, you'd start to get the picture. But in 2000-2002 it was the cheapest four-wheeler you could hire in Bali, so I was stuck with it for a couple of holidays. It wouldn't go more than 45mph, and even then I got targeted by the local police for not having a Balinese driving licence. The bribe was many thousands of rupiahs (that actually worked out at about £13), and the receiving officer had the good grace to write his mobile number on the top of the receipt to give me an indemnity if I ever got stopped again. I did get stopped again – the next day, at the same place, by another cop – but, happily, my new-found friend spotted this, and confirmed his honesty by sending me on my way.

FLAT TYRE RATING: 🛞 🛞 🛞 🛞 🛞

Suzuki X90
1996-1998

SEEING HAIRDRESSERS blinging up their Vitaras, Suzuki thought it would be a whizzo idea to chuck out the back seats and construct this crock of crap. Even four layers of St Tropez fake tan and a bleached and lacquered barnet could not compensate. A clown's car for people who wanted to drive around looking ridiculous.

GEORGE SAYS: Is Honest nuts? Well yes, of course he is, I've always known that, but while the X90 may have looked ridiculous it was actually quite a sweet little number. Fair enough the image was all wrong but it actually drove okay, and my little lad, who was just 10 years old at the time, loved standing in the space between the flatback boot and the back seats. Okay the ride was far too bouncy, it lost all sense of road holding in the wet, the boot lid actually cracked the back of the drivers head if it was shut by someone else, and the wind noise became unpleasant over 50mph, but apart from that … hmm, Honest is not so mad after all.

FLAT TYRE RATING: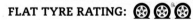

Suzuki Kizashi
2012-2014

THE NAME Kizashi is Japanese for "A sign of great things to come." So why the hell did Suzuki give that moniker to one of the biggest duds it's ever made? In fact, why did it even make it? To say that the Kizashi was overpriced, under-equipped, slow, noisy and thirsty would be like saying that the Kray twins were just a couple of naughty boys. Okay, it doesn't sound remotely appealing, and it wasn't, but believe me the Kizashi was all those things, only much, much worse. When I first drove it with a mate, we held a guessing game over the size of its engine and its price. Finally, we both agreed that it was a 1.4-litre and it was probably around the £15,000 mark. We were as hopelessly wrong as the Kizashi was terrible. This overweight insult (it was 1625kg) had a giant, but vastly underpowered, 2.4-litre engine, and a European price-tag of £21,995. From then on the story actually went even further downhill. The interior was totally bland, made worse by dull dials and switchgear, its CVT (constantly variable transmission) gearbox whined in agony as you attempted to drag the car along, it gulped down petrol like a drunk at a free beer festival, and that was before you attached a caravan, sorry anchor, to it. Yep, it had four-wheel-drive and was supposed to appeal to outdoor folk, only the words appeal and Kizashi should never have appeared in the same sentence. Suzuki sold it in Europe for three years, from 2012 to 2014, and sold just 1905 of these cess pits. In its last year, until it was dropped in October, a mere 281 people bought one. And that's across the whole of Europe. You'd think there would be more idiots than that out of a population of 745 million. Obviously, few people are actually that stupid.

FLAT TYRE RATING: 🛞 🛞 🛞 🛞

Tata Nano
2008

THE DIRT-CHEAP people's car that the people didn't want. After all, why buy an ungainly egg-on-wheels with no bootlid when a motorbike is more parkable and a lot more fun, and for a few more rupees you could have a proper little Maruti Suzuki anyway? Can you imagine the purgatory of travelling a thousand miles across India crammed inside one of these horrors, together with wife, three kids and mother-in-law, and without air-conditioning? Neither could Indians, who kept saving and went out and bought Dacia Dusters instead.

FLAT TYRE RATING:

Tata Nano (see previous page)

Tata Safari
1998-2015

DESCRIBING THE horror that was driving a Tata Safari is like surveying the aftermath of a war scene. The only place I should have taken this wreck of a motor was straight to the knacker's yard, but if that had involved going up a hill I doubt it would have got there. Such was the racket coming from its ancient, creaking, 2.0-litre diesel, that it sounded like a tractor with barely the power to drag along its protesting frame. Its so-called seats left me in constant pain, a trim panel around its ancient 60s switches fell off, as did one of the rear door handles. The interior lights refused to switch off, the engine immobiliser light kept going on and off, the clutch pedal would suddenly become so stiff it felt like a cat had crawled in and got stuck underneath

it. It had the turning circle of a super-tanker in a canal, which rendered it completely impossible to drive in some streets, where a straightforward six-point turn at night would wake up the entire town. It bounced about like a boat in a gale if you hit so much as a small bump, and I concluded that, even if it had been £14,495 cheaper, I still wouldn't have wanted one. That was how much it would have cost new. It was vile beyond belief.

FLAT TYRE RATING:
🛞🛞🛞🛞🛞

151

Toyota Avensis
2003-2009

THIS CAME from the era when every Toyota didn't just have to have a logo of a bull, it had to look like one. It had expensive multi-link rear suspension, but was designed for comfort and longevity rather than performance. There was an unfathomable sat nav, with no map display on the dash. The original belt cam 2.0-litre D-4D was reliable, and turned a solid car into a stolid one. But the petrol engines had bore liner problems and Toyota extended the warranty. Then the company developed a pair of 2.0-litre and 2.2-litre chain cam D-4Ds that had cylinder head problems. So, though you could forgive the Avensis for its stolidity because it was reliable, it wasn't particularly, so you couldn't.

FLAT TYRE RATING:

Toyota Alphard
2002

THE CONVEYANCE of choice of Far Eastern gangsters and politicians (hard to tell the difference). Gratuitously hideous and continuously vulgarised over the years to make it the nadir of naffness. Though quite comfortable and practical as a chauffeur-driven businessman's express, in which meetings, beatings and other things could take place behind privacy glass and curtains, the outward appearance of this monstrosity speaks volumes of the pretensions of its owners.

FLAT TYRE RATING: 🛞🛞🛞

Toyota Fortuner
2003

NAMED AFTER the pungent cigarettes that used to give Spanish airports their distinctive aroma, the Fortuner has been weapon of choice for the very worst of Thai drivers for 13 years. It looms immensely on the twin-rail chassis of the Toyota HiLux pickup, but sports a gargantuan MPV body with seats for five plus two McDonalds and KFC stuffed children. The turning circle is akin to an HGV's, so to make a 'U-turn' requires up to three lanes, or up to four if the driver just wants to cut across everything and park. Fortuners have automatic right of way everywhere except against Bangkok City buses, that are bigger and so bashed up anyway that the drivers simply don't care. Imagine 1990s Range Rover mentality, multiply it by ten and add a quadruple helping of BMW X6 driver attitude, and you will understand why you need to watch out for these monsters and stay well clear.

FLAT TYRE RATING:

Vauxhall Corsa
1993-2000

HILARIOUSLY, THIS nasty little car built on the outskirts of Zaragoza, was originally called the 'No Va' in Britain, which translated from Spanish to 'Doesn't Go'. How the workforce must have chortled as they left their uneaten bocadillos in the door bottoms, and otherwise sabotaged RHD Corsas destined for the UK with ridiculous 'Doesn't Go' badges riveted to their prematurely rusting bootlids. Quite why the *Max Power* boy racers took to them is beyond comprehension, or perhaps because comprehension wasn't their strong point. Coarsers had a disquieting habit of cracking half way up their B pillars that didn't instil hirers of holiday rentals with confidence. Their GF50 plastic timing belt pulleys failed until GM started fitting chain cam 1.0 and 1.2 engines. And it was the car that introduced us to the execrable Easychronic automated manual transmissions.

FLAT TYRE RATING:

Vauxhall Vectra
1995-2002

THE REHASHED Cavalier that Vauxhall built to compete with the Mondeo and, though it fixed the steering rack to the subframe instead of to the bulkhead, it had so much understeer you had to predict where the next corner would be. I vividly recall having to turn in to Redgate at Donington at least ten metres before the corner started. The pointlessly pointy little mirrors made it difficult to see Mondeos overtaking you. Police, who got them at a 60% discount, complained bitterly about that. The Vectra even starred as the Dursley's appropriately dismal family car in the very first 'Harry Potter' movie. Oddly, though, despite an early rash of ABS failures at £1800 a pop, Vectras settled down to be quite respectable superbangers that didn't deteriorate quite as badly after 15 years as contemporary Mondeos.

GEORGE ADDS: The Vectra was seriously lagging behind the Ford Mondeo when Vauxhall brought out the second generation of its second choice repmobile in 2002. They'd promised us "A car that will be more than a rival" to the Mondeo, and gave it a new look, new chassis, new engines, new interior and new equipment. This just had to be good; even Jeremy Clarkson came on the car's launch in Spain, and no wonder. You see, by then Clarkson's hate of all things Vauxhall, and especially the Vectra, had become legendary, and once again Vauxhall's latest effort proved him to be right. The second stab at the Vectra was a massive let-down to say the least. I remember collaring one of their executives at lunch and telling him: "You promised us a totally different car. This is just as bad as the last one. It's nothing like the Mondeo." Needless to say he just smiled and walked away. What could he say? The car still handled like a jelly, had the power of a used bullet, and had switches that were so confusing that, for most of the launch, journalists were driving along with their indicators flashing or their wipers scraping over dry windscreens. It was awful. The only happy person who came home from that debacle was Jeremy Clarkson.

FLAT TYRE RATING: 🛞

Volkswagen Golf R32
2003

VW PUT so much stuff into the R32 that it forgot about its unfortunate drivers. There was a massive 3.2-litre V6 wedged under its bonnet, with 235hp mated to the slickest of boxes that made just changing gear pure delight. Trouble was, it was so fast that I spent most of my time ignoring it and just changing from second gear to sixth at 70mph. There has to be a bit more to a car than sheer speed, and VW ignored everything else. That's why drivers spent most of their time sitting in a seat that was so uncomfortable their legs could barely reach the pedals, even on its lowest setting. Worse still, it had a raised lip at the front of it so your legs felt like they were dangling over the edge. Its silly little instruments were, for the most part, unreadable because they were tiny and positioned so low down under the dash you had to take your eyes off the road if you needed to adjust anything. Its trip computer refused to tell you how many miles were left in the petrol tank and, given that it was called the Golf, it seemed strange that there wasn't enough room in the boot for golf clubs. It was nice for the first ten minutes, but impracticality overtook speed, and for the whole week it drove me nuts.

HJ ADDS: I had the painful experience of driving a special edition Golf about this time. I thought it was the Edition 30, based on the GTI, to celebrate 30 years of Golf. The problem was that the seats had been designed for six-foot six-inch Germans, whose shoulders came out of their bodies above the side bolsters, or skinny women whose shoulders fitted inside the side bolsters. But five-foot nine-inch me was turned into Quasimodo by the things, so could not drive it more than ten miles without suffering the kind of back injury that ambulance-chasing lawyers specialise in.

FLAT TYRE RATING: 🛞🛞🛞

Faultswagen Golf Mk VI
2009-2012

THE MORE cars you sell, and the more you sustain a myth of reliability, the more complaints you're going to get when buyers don't actually experience it. And the record for complaints at honestjohn.co.uk so far stands at 130 for the 2009 to 2012 Volkswagen Golf Mk VI, a car for which the myth was sustained to a deluded public by TV advertising. VW wasn't allowed to continue using the 1983 "Few things in life are as reliable" line from the famous David Bailey/Paula Hamilton commercial because it couldn't be proven, so it resorted to implication in the sickeningly smug "It's not a Golf" campaign. Decent enough to drive. Nice illusion of quality from things like a velour lined glovebox. But the list of problems kept mounting until the final catastrophe of the US Emissions Defeat software that proved they'd been lying all along.

FLAT TYRE RATING: 🛞🛞🛞🛞

Faultswagen Golf Mk VI
2009-2012

THE MORE cars you sell, and the more you sustain a myth of reliability, the more complaints you're going to get when buyers don't actually experience it. And the record for complaints at honestjohn.co.uk so far stands at 130 for the 2009 to 2012 Volkswagen Golf Mk VI, a car for which the myth was sustained to a deluded public by TV advertising. VW wasn't allowed to continue using the 1983 "Few things in life are as reliable" line from the famous David Bailey/Paula Hamilton commercial because it couldn't be proven, so it resorted to implication in the sickeningly smug "It's not a Golf" campaign. Decent enough to drive. Nice illusion of quality from things like a velour lined glovebox. But the list of problems kept mounting until the final catastrophe of the US Emissions Defeat software that proved they'd been lying all along.

FLAT TYRE RATING: 🛞🛞🛞🛞

Faultswagon Passat
2005-2011

IT SEEMED that VW couldn't make up its mind how to position the engine in the Passat. First it was longitudinal, overhanging the front axle like an Audi. Then, from 1988 to 1997, it went transverse, like a Golf. From 1997 to 2005 it was back to longitudinal, and that was probably the best Passat ever, after which it hit its nadir with the once again transverse-engined Passat B6. There is almost nothing to recommend about this car, apart from the optional lockable fold down rear seatbacks. It was the first mainstream VW to adopt electromechanical parking brakes that were prone to water ingress, and cost £600-a-side to replace. The only reliable engine was the old 1.9TDI PD because the 2.0TDI had a dodgy oil pump drive, which is like a human being with an unreliable heart. DSG 'automatic' transmissions were slow to respond from a standstill (there was even a full scale recall). The brake sensor in the ABS/ESP module failed, leading greedy VW dealers to attempt to stiff owners with a £1900 fix on cars just out of warranty. The accumulation of complaints just kept on accumulating. And on. And on.

FLAT TYRE RATING: 🛞🛞🛞🛞

Index

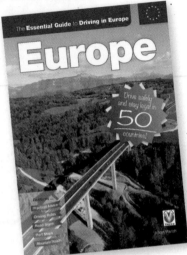
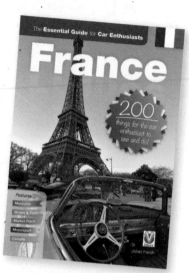